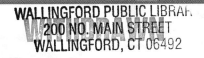

Medieval Feasts and Banquets

Food, Drink, and Celebration in the Middle Ages

Tehmina Bhote

rosen central™

The Rosen Publishing Group, Inc., New York

Published in 2004 by The Rosen Publishing Group, Inc.
29 East 21st Street, New York, NY 10010

Library of Congress Cataloging-in-Publication Data

Bhote, Tehmina.
Medieval feasts and banquets: food, drink, and celebration in the middle ages/Tehmina Bhote.—1st ed.
    p. cm.—(The library of the Middle Ages)
Includes bibliographical references and index.
ISBN 0-8239-3993-6 (library binding)
1. Gastronomy. 2. Food habits. 3. Dinners and dining.
I. Title. II. Series.
TX631.B49 2003
394.1'094'0902—dc21

                                        2002154250

Manufactured in the United States of America

Table of Contents

This calendar from a fifteenth-century French illuminated manuscript shows agricultural activities appropriate to each month of the year. There are scenes showing the spreading of manure on the fields, the pruning of vines, the shearing of sheep, the harvesting and gathering of wheat, the sowing of seeds, the crushing of grapes, and the slaughtering of pigs.

The Production and Distribution of Food

Imagine a place where people had not heard of potatoes, tomatoes, chilies, chocolate, or corn. Medieval Europeans had not yet discovered the Americas, where these foods came from. There was no electricity, refrigeration, or modern stoves, and there weren't any of the electrical gadgets that many people use to prepare food today.

This book is about what Europeans ate and drank during the Middle Ages, both every day and during times of celebration and at feasts and banquets. Feasts and banquets were also times of great entertainment and ceremony, enjoyed by all classes of people from the peasant and the town merchant to the bishop, noble, king, and queen.

Most of the population of medieval Europe were farmers, both men and women. Children also worked on farms. Fields, gardens, and orchards were the source of most food and drink. The food that was produced was also used as money. It was exchanged for other food or goods, or used to pay rent, or a "tithe," a tax paid to the church.

Medieval farmers, who were called peasants, were tenant farmers and usually worked the land owned by the lord of the local manor or castle. Some were free people. Others had no choice but to work on their lord's land. The lands owned by nobles and bishops around their manor houses and castles were called estates. In return for working the land, the peasants would give the lord of the manor a portion of all the food that was produced. Sometimes village farmers shared common land that did not belong to a noble's estate. The food produced here could be shared between the villagers or sold at a local market. Monasteries had their own land that was farmed by monks and nuns.

How Food Was Grown

The farming year traditionally began at the start of spring, when work outside started in the fields and gardens. There was no motorized machinery to help with farming. People and animals did all the work in the fields. Oxen—and later, horses—were used to pull heavy plows to prepare the fields for sowing. The type of crop that was sown in each field was changed every year as part of a system of crop rotation. One field was always left empty with nothing growing on it. This was the "fallow field," where animals were left to graze. The manure produced by the animals was used to fertilize the field for the following year. This was a vitally important method of farming in northern Europe, where growing seasons were short and soils were poor. Nutrients had to be restored to the soil in order to grow a successful crop the next year.

Grains such as wheat, rye, and barley were planted. Peas and beans were also grown. In colder climates, oats

From a fifteenth-century French manuscript, this composite scene of medieval rural life shows peasants digging and planting, shearing sheep, and harvesting apples.

were grown. Wheat and rye were used to make flour for bread. Barley was used to brew ale. Cereal crops were used for animal fodder as well as human food. In the warmer parts of Europe such as southern France, Italy, and Spain, grapes were grown in vineyards to make wine. Olive trees were also grown in warmer regions. Olives were very important because olive oil was used both for cooking and for fuel in oil lamps. Fruit trees were grown in orchards. In colder climates, mainly apples and pears were grown. In warmer parts of Europe, peaches, lemons, and oranges were also cultivated. Some vegetables were grown in small gardens. Here leeks, onions, garlic, cabbages, and lettuces were the main crops. Herbs were used for cooking and for medicines. Parsley, fennel, celery, mint, mustard, and coriander were commonly grown in medieval gardens.

It was extremely important for crops to be protected against weeds, birds, snails, slugs, and insect pests. Special tools were made to help farmers get rid of weeds. When the seeds were first sown in the fields and gardens, it was vital that birds were prevented from eating them. Scaring away the birds was usually a good job for children, and they often ran around the fields with slings to do this. Soot from fireplaces was sometimes scattered around fields and gardens to prevent snails and slugs from eating crops.

Animals such as cows, goats, and sheep were milked regularly. Although many people did not drink milk, it was used to make butter and cheese. Geese and chickens produced the eggs that were a key part of the diet for all people in medieval society. In autumn, swine were sent into the forests to forage for the acorns and other nuts that fell from the trees. Eating

From the *Luttrell Psalter*, a book of religious psalms written by Sir Geoffrey Luttrell of Irnham, England, around 1340, this marginal illustration shows two farmers using oxen to pull a plow.

nuts fattened the pigs so there would be more meat on them when they were slaughtered. Bees were also kept in man-made hives for their honey. Beeswax was used to make candles. Many nobles kept doves, swans, and peacocks on their land. These birds were eaten, too, especially at feasts.

Traditionally, livestock animals that were to be eaten were slaughtered at the end of autumn. But animals were also slaughtered for meat at other times of the year, especially for fresh meat for feasts and banquets. Meat would last longer if it was smoked or preserved in salt. The fat from animals was made into tallow to make candles.

This fifteenth-century Flemish illustration shows plowing and the sowing of seeds. The farmer here uses horses rather than oxen.

Hunting, Fishing, and Foraging

There were complicated laws about hunting in the Middle Ages, which usually meant that a person had to obtain special permission to hunt in the forests or marshes that normally formed part of the lord's or king's estate. Hunting was generally allowed only for wealthy people and the nobility. Hunting was a good source of fresh meat. There were no guns, and hunting dogs were used to chase and kill wild animals like deer and boars. Birds of prey like falcons and hawks were trained to kill wild birds like pigeons and partridges. Smaller animals such as rabbits and ground birds like pheasants were caught in nets or traps. Although peasants and poorer people were not normally able to hunt legally, they did catch small animals like rabbits and pheasants. This was called poaching.

Fishing was done in lakes, ponds, rivers, and the open sea. Villages and towns that were close to the coast or to a river normally provided the fish and shellfish for the local community and beyond. Fish such as herring, pike, salmon, cod, and anchovies were caught, as well as eels, oysters, and crayfish. Methods for fishing included the traditional rod, line, and baited hook; large nets when fishing at sea; and fish traps called weirs used in rivers. Oysters were raked up from shallow sea and riverbeds. Wealthy nobles often had large lakes or ponds on their estates that were well stocked with fish. Fishing in these lakes also required permission from the owner, and anyone caught fishing illegally was punished. Fish, like meat, was also preserved by salting and smoking. Whales and seals were hunted for food, especially to supply royal banquets.

Medieval people went foraging in the woods and forests to obtain food such as nuts, wild berries, mushrooms, and wild honey. Foraging was an important method for obtaining food when supplies were low. People in the mountainous regions of France and Italy foraged for chestnuts. They were an important part of their diet.

Obtaining Food and Drink

For people living in the countryside, both peasant farmers and rich nobles, most food and drink was obtained from the land they lived on or from small village markets. Grain had to be taken to a local miller to be ground into flour. The miller would take some of the grain as payment. There were permanent markets in large towns and cities as well as international fairs on "feast days," where merchants from far away came to trade their goods. Food could also be obtained from wandering sellers, both men and women, who sold goods from house to house or in market centers. Some merchants in towns sold food and drink from their own houses where their goods were stored.

Most people who lived in towns relied on their local market or shop to provide them with food, which usually came from the surrounding countryside. Richer townspeople who had their own gardens could grow their own vegetables and fruit. Animals like cows and sheep could also be hired for the use of their milk. Nobles and rich merchants had large rooms under their houses to store their food and drink. Manors and castles had very large pantries, where meats and jars of preserved foods were stored. Cats were kept in the pantry to chase away rats and mice that might spoil the food. Wine and

This fifteenth-century French illustration depicts a man fishing in a stream with a large net.

ale were stored in a "bottlery" or "buttery" in large wooden barrels. Rich merchants who lived in large houses in town often had special vaults underground to store wine.

Markets, Shops, and Merchants

Port cities and towns on major trading routes enjoyed the widest variety of food, spices, and drinks. People from around the local countryside, other towns, and from overseas came to buy and sell their goods at the big markets held at these places.

A special grant had to be obtained for holding a market or fair, either from the king or queen, or from the ruling elite of a city, who had certain rights to govern affairs in its region. An example is the grant given by Otto the Great, the Holy Roman emperor, to the bishop of a German town called Wyddenbrugge in the year 952. The local authorities were also given the right to mint their own coins and collect taxes from visiting merchants and traders.

Markets were busy and chaotic places. Everyday foods, as well as more exotic luxury foods, were sold at the market. The common foods included bread, flour, eggs, butter, cheese, and salt, as well as the meat, vegetables, herbs, and fruit that were in season. In large cities such as London and Paris, certain markets were devoted to selling one type of food, like the fish market, the meat market, and the corn market. Real corn did not appear in Europe until the discovery of the New World, but at this time "corn" was used to describe other grains like wheat and barley.

Spices from the East, such as pepper, saffron, ginger, nutmeg, and cloves, were used when special meals were prepared

A hunting party returns from the hunt in this sixteenth-century Flemish manuscript. A deer can be seen slung over a horse. Note the use of a team of hunting dogs in the lower left.

oie li uocem eius audieritis : no
bdurare coida ueftra
it in irritacione : fecundum oie

A fourteenth-century manuscript illumination depicts peasants harrowing. Harrowing follows sowing and involves covering and smoothing the soil over the seeds. A boy with a sling and stones follows the farmer to scare away birds that might eat the seeds.

for feasts and banquets. These could be bought from the spice merchant at a market. Sugar, rice, rosewater, dried fruit (like apricots and dates), and nuts (like pistachios) could also be bought from the spice merchant. Such goods came from all over the known world, from North Africa, Persia, Arabia, India, and China.

Merchants obtained foods from overseas by sending ships along the trade routes to the East, exchanging goods from home such as wool, timber, and metal for exotic foods and spices. Merchants in northern Europe imported fine wines from France and Italy. In the medieval English port of Southampton, many rich merchants kept very large wine vaults under their houses that stored much of the wine that was sent to other parts of the country, even to the king and queen.

In towns and cities, bread could be bought ready-made from the baker's shop. There were also butchers' shops and fishmongers in towns where fresh and preserved meat could be obtained. At "cookshops" people could buy ready-made foods such as pies and sauces. For people who did not make their own ale and wine, ale could be bought from the market or at an ale shop or brewery, and wine from a wine merchant's warehouse. Travelers, such as trading merchants and pilgrims, could obtain food and drink on their journey at inns and taverns where they could also rest for the night. Pilgrims were able to go to monasteries along the pilgrim routes where monks and nuns would provide food, drink, and shelter.

Shopping

The Goodman of Paris was a merchant in medieval France. When he married his young wife, he wrote a manual for her around 1393 that included advice about what to buy when shopping for a large feast. For example, he suggested that at the butcher's shop she was to buy bacon, half a sheep for the soup, a leg bone of a cow to make broth, and a "hefty leg of venison."

Dame Alice de Bryene held a New Year's banquet in 1413 in her manor in eastern England. Her household accounts show that there were two hundred meals in her banquet, and although most of the food and drink was obtained from her own land and pantry, she had to purchase beef, veal, young pigs, and twelve gallons of milk. She would have been able to obtain these from the village market or from another estate. Her accounts also show that she sometimes went to the market herself for food, spices, and salt. This was rare for a noblewoman.

Food, Famine, and Cooking

edieval people usually ate two meals a day—a main meal called dinner after a morning's work and a light meal called supper at the end of a day's work. A light breakfast may have been eaten after waking at dawn.

Upper orders of society, such as the nobility, bishops, and wealthy merchants, could afford to eat fresh meat and fish regularly. Peasants and less wealthy people generally ate meat and fish only on special occasions. Unlike today, when most food can be bought all year round, medieval people relied on what was available at different times of the year. In winter, preserved foods were eaten.

Staple Foods

Staple foods are basic foods that people eat regularly. The main staple of medieval people, whether in the town or country, was "pottage," a thick soup. Pottage was usually made from boiling together beans or peas with whatever vegetables were available at the time. Peasants sometimes added scraps of meat or fish that were available and

This fifteenth-century French manuscript illumination shows a peasant knocking down acorns from oak trees to feed his pigs.

affordable. The wealthier people in society could afford a wider variety of ingredients, and they used fresh fish and meat in their pottages as well as spices like pepper. Herbs like parsley could be used to give more flavor. Wealthier people in medieval Italy added pasta to their dishes. Often the pottage would be kept simmering for days at a time over the fire. Ingredients could be added to the pottage when needed. An important staple for people who lived in hilly and mountainous areas in central France and Italy was chestnuts. This is because it was more difficult to grow grain in mountainous areas. Chestnuts were eaten boiled up in a form of pottage and could also be ground into a coarse flour to make heavy breads and cakes. Wheat, barley, or oats were boiled to make porridge.

Bread was also a staple food. Most people ate dark breads made from rye or other coarse flour. White bread was normally eaten at feasts and banquets. It was seen as a symbol of wealth. For people who kept cows, sheep, and goats, milk was available to make cheese, which could be eaten with bread for supper. Eggs were eaten by those who could get them. They were a good source of protein, especially for those who could not get meat. Those who could afford meat and fish regularly boiled them up in stews or roasted small birds, like capons, on a spit. The main meat of the less wealthy peasants was pork, usually in the form of bacon. Two medieval English writers, Geoffrey Chaucer and William Langland, who wrote in the 1300s, described the food of ordinary people in the stories they wrote. Brown bread, bacon, sometimes an egg, cheese, and beans are examples of the foods they mention in their tales.

There is not much evidence about what medieval babies and children ate. Some medieval documents say that young children were fed on a porridge made from boiling oats, wheat, or another grain in milk. As children were expected to work at a much younger age than today, they would probably have eaten the same food as their parents.

Staple Drinks

Water was generally not drunk on its own during the Middle Ages. Rivers and water supplies in towns were likely to be polluted with rubbish and waste. Unless people were too poor to buy other drinks, water was avoided. It could cause fatal diseases such as cholera. Most people's staple drinks were wine and ale. Ale was generally drunk in the northern parts of Europe and wine in the southern parts. Even children drank wine and ale, but it was generally made with more water and less alcohol than today's wine and beer.

Both ale and wine could be drunk hot, too, sometimes with spices or herbs added. Adding spices was called mulling. Although milk was available, it was generally used for cooking by the wealthy. Medieval documents tell us that milk was viewed as a drink only for young children, the old, and the sick. However, buttermilk, the milky liquid that remained when butter was churned, was drunk by less wealthy people. In some parts of Europe, cider, an alcoholic drink made from apples, was a staple drink when apples were in season. Another drink called mead was a wine made from honey. Mead was mainly drunk in England and the region now known as Germany.

Bakers at work, from a Book of Hours written around AD 1500

Famine and Bad Food

A bad harvest was a devastating blow for medieval people. Some people were driven to eat the food they grew as fodder for their animals. Flour for foods such as bread could be made with beans when grain was in short supply. A shortage of food caused high prices, so the rich managed best during famines, as they had the money to buy what little there was available. The rich also had large stores of food and drink to fall back upon. Some churches and hospitals tried to help the poorer people in times of famine by giving them food and drink as charity, called alms. A chronicler tells the story of a food riot in the Italian city of Siena in 1329. When a hospital in the city was giving out alms during the famine, there were so many people desperate to get hold of bread that the hospital shut its doors, as it could not cope with the demand. The hungry people ran to the main square of the city, where grain and bread were being sold, and ransacked the market for whatever they could lay their hands on. They shouted, "Mercy! We're dying of hunger."

People also became ill or died from eating bad food. Meat and fish from markets could easily start rotting, or meals could be made from rotten ingredients. Wine and ale could also go sour and cause illness. It was up to the person buying the food to check it. There was no government agency monitoring food quality, and the germ theory of disease was not understood. Sometimes those making the food would deliberately use cheaper ingredients or additives to save money. Court records show people accusing bakers of selling bread with sand, dirt, and cobwebs in it. Innkeepers who sold wine and ale were also taken to court when found to sell low quality drinks. Saint Anthony's fire, or ergotism, was a disease that afflicted people who ate bread that was made from moldy grain. Ergotism could cause terrible fevers and delirium.

Preparing and Preserving Food

Most medieval people cooked their food themselves and made their drinks themselves. Wealthy people and nobles employed professional people to make food and drinks for them, especially for feasts and banquets. Most people learned how to cook food and make drinks from their elders.

In the days before refrigerators and freezers, preserving food was essential. Salting was the most common way that

This fifteenth-century manuscript illumination depicts peasants harvesting grapes. In the background is the Chateau de Saumur.

meat and fish could be preserved. Beef and pork were covered in fine granules of salt. This was called dry-curing. Brining was a more popular method. Brine is made by dissolving salt in water. Fish and meat could be preserved in brine, especially herring. Butter and cheese lasted longer if salt was added when they were made.

Smoking meat and fish was another method of preserving them. They had to be salted in brine first and then hung over an open fire indoors to be dried and smoked. This was done to pork to make bacon. In hot climates in southern Europe, food could be dried by exposing it to the sun. Fish, meat, and vegetables could also be pickled in vinegar and stored in pottery jars.

Cooking

Open fires provided the means to cook food as well as a source of heat for most people. Peasants and less wealthy people cooked on the fire in the center of their houses. There was little ventilation and there were no chimneys, so it could get very smoky inside. Food was also cooked outside, as it was safer. A fire inside the house could easily spread and burn the house down. In large households there would be an open fire in a large kitchen built of stone. The cooks would have had many pots, pans, spoons, and knives to cook with and a large wooden table on which to prepare fancy foods.

Pottage and anything that required boiling was made in large pots or cauldrons made of iron or brass. The pots were hung over an open fire or placed on top of a metal trivet that sat on the fire. The fire was fueled by wood or charcoal. Meat could be roasted on a spit over the fire, but this was expensive, as it used up a lot of wood. Meat and fish could also be grilled on a grid of metal bars called a grid-iron. For those without bread ovens in their homes, villages and towns had communal ovens where bread could be baked for a fee. In towns and cities people could pay a baker to bake their bread for them. There were also shops that would roast meat for people.

Eggs, beans, meat, and fish were fried on top of the fire in pans. In southern Europe, olive oil was used for frying. In other parts of Europe animal fat was used if it was available and affordable.

Brewing Ale and Making Wine

Ale was made with grain, mainly barley. The barley was "malted," that is, left to germinate or start growing in water. The grain was then roasted slowly to stop the seed from growing further. This malt was crushed and boiled in water. After the liquid had cooled, yeast was added. As the yeast reacted with the sugars in the malt, it changed them into alcohol. The ale was stored in wooden barrels. As ale went sour quickly, it had to be made regularly. In the later Middle Ages, a type of herb called hops was added, which helped preserve the ale for a longer time. Ale with hops is called beer.

Wine was used as a substitute for water and in cooking meals for feasts. Wine that had become sour was used as vinegar. Wine was made by first crushing the grapes, which required lots of people to tread on them with their feet in large stone or wooden tubs to press the juice out. The skins from the crushed grapes then floated to the top. Usually, if white

A man is roasting barley to make beer in this fourteenth-century Italian treatise on medicine. Wine and beer were preferred drinks because much of Europe's water was not safe to drink in the Middle Ages.

wine was to be made, the skins were removed from the liquid. If red wine was being made, the skins were left to give the wine a dark red color. The skins of the grapes had yeast on them, and so the liquid started fermenting. The wine was stored in large wooden barrels usually made from oak.

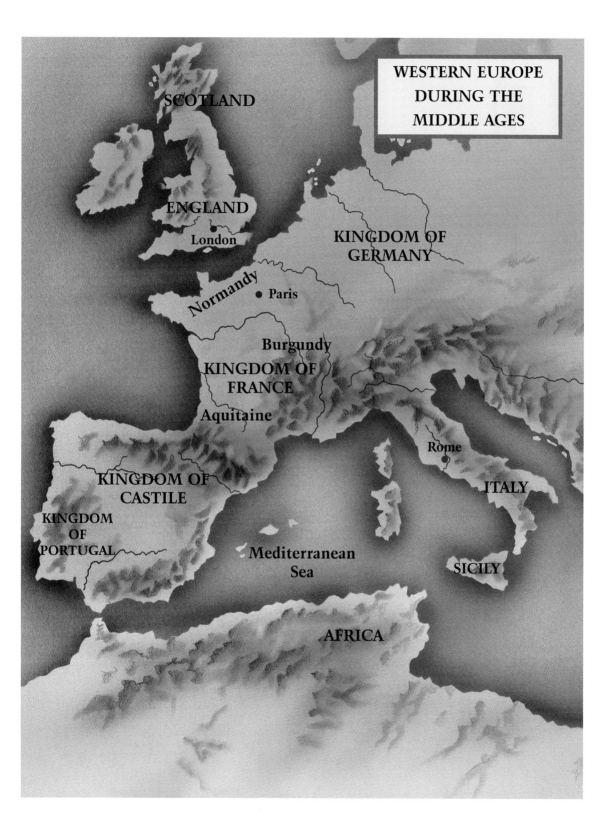

WESTERN EUROPE
DURING THE
MIDDLE AGES

SCOTLAND

ENGLAND
London

KINGDOM OF
GERMANY

Normandy
Paris

Burgundy

KINGDOM OF
FRANCE

Aquitaine

Rome

KINGDOM OF
CASTILE

ITALY

KINGDOM
OF
PORTUGAL

Mediterranean
Sea

SICILY

AFRICA

Eating and Drinking

I n the Middle Ages, the main meals of dinner and supper would have been eaten in the home. Monks or nuns would eat in the monastery or nunnery. Peasants and the poor had very small homes by modern standards. Families would sit on benches or stools around a wooden rectangular table near the fire or on the floor to eat. When it was warm and dry outside, people may have eaten outdoors, near their houses. For people who had no room to host a feast in their homes, tables could be set up in the open air or in the village square, and a temporary shelter could be built from wooden posts and cloth.

The great halls of medieval manors, castles, and palaces were enormous rooms with high ceilings. The great hall was the most important room in the manor house, since it was where deals were made and feasts and banquets were held. Walls were painted in bright colors or were hung with beautiful tapestries and fine silk and woollen drapes. Tapestries often told stories in pictures or featured religious scenes from the Bible. Floors were inlaid with expensive tiles often showing the family's coat of arms. Sometimes even the great halls

celum + terram
Celum celi domino : terram autem
dedit filiis hominum

This kitchen scene is from the *Luttrell Psalter*. Servants are cutting up meat, pouring drinks from earthenware jugs into cups, and carrying food to the lord's table.

were not big enough, and temporary halls had to be built just for a special banquet.

The utensils people used to eat and drink with said a lot about how wealthy they were. Less wealthy people used utensils made of locally available wood. Spoons and cups could even be cut out of animal horns. Larger items like jugs and pots could be made of earthenware, a type of pottery, and painted with patterns. Objects made of metal and glass were much more expensive and could only be purchased by rich people. At some royal banquets, the important guests ate with utensils made of gold and silver and were served from large platters and jugs decorated with precious jewels and engravings.

People ate with spoons and with their fingers. A small knife was used to cut up pieces of meat. Most people carried a small knife around with them as a useful tool and used it when eating. Table forks were not used. People's everyday food like pottage would have been eaten from wooden or earthenware bowls. Wealthy people may have used metal bowls. The same bowl could also be used to drink ale. At feasts, large, thick slices of bread called trenchers were used as plates. After the feast the trenchers were either soaked in gravy and eaten up or collected to feed the poor.

Everyday drinks were generally drunk from wooden or earthenware cups. Ale was kept in leather tankards. "Mazers" were small, shallow bowls used for drinking wine and ale. They could be made of wood, such as maple, or metal. Goblets and glasses were generally used to drink wine. Medieval Venice was known for making fine and colorful glass.

At feasts and banquets, only the host and important guests were served by servants. Others helped themselves from large platters of meat and fish, dishes of pottage, sauces from saucers, and oil and vinegar from cruets. Table fountains were like pieces of art in the shape of castles with turrets and towers. They had many spouts from which different drinks could be poured through pipes.

As people ate with their fingers, it was necessary to clean them before and during the meal. At feasts and banquets, a servant would pour water on the hands of important guests from special containers called ewers or aquamaniles. Sometimes the water would be scented with perfumes. Everyone was given large cloth napkins to wipe their hands during the meal. Ewers could also be made from precious metals and adorned with

A fifteenth-century German watercolor portrays a cook at work.

jewels. The saltcellar was a tabletop container for salt, and it was usually in the shape of a ship. It was an important symbol on the feast table. Important guests sat "above the salt," and less important guests sat "below the salt."

Good Manners

Medieval books of courtesy contained advice about how people should behave while eating and drinking. Although most people could not read, they would have been brought up to know good manners. Most books about manners said that no one should start eating or drinking until the head of the household or the host and the important guests at a feast had started. Everyone had to wash hands before starting to eat. You were not supposed to speak while you were chewing your food or to dip your fingers in the food too much. Elbows had to be kept off the table. Burping, arguing, and loud laughing at the table were bad manners.

At the wedding banquet of an Italian merchant's daughter, Ginevra, in the 1300s, the bride was careful to eat beforehand and did not touch the meal at the banquet. When the servant came round with the washing bowl for her, the water remained clear, and the guests praised her good manners. No one really knows how far such manners were followed. As feasts and banquets were important occasions in almost everyone's lives, people would be expected to be on their best behavior.

Feasts and Banquets

A special day in the calendar or an important event in someone's life was expected to be celebrated with a feast. For ordinary

Peasants thresh and sift grain in this eleventh-century English calendar. The short growing season in northern Europe produced poor-quality crops and low yields. Tasteless foods created a desire for spices.

folk it provided a time of rest and enjoyment from their daily work. Royalty and nobles could display their wealth and power by sitting in the most important place at the banquet table and by providing expensive and exotic foods to the guests. The guests were expected to marvel at such rich and wonderful food and drink to show their appreciation of the host.

Most people in medieval Europe were Christians. At certain times of the year, Christians were expected to fast, (that is, to refrain from eating), or to eat only certain types of food. Three days of every week—Wednesday, Friday, and Saturday—were fast days or fish days when meat or dairy

These men make ropes and nets for a hunt, in an early-fifteenth-century French manuscript.

products could not be eaten. It was believed that not eating meat was good for your soul. About fifty days in the year were times of religious celebration called feast days. A handbook for priests written in 1385 said that the local priest should announce the feast days and fast days to his community. Some people felt that because ducks and other birds swam on the water, they could be thought of as fish and therefore eaten on fish days. Many laypeople did not observe all the fast days. The church thought that feasts were good occasions for people to enjoy food and a chance for them to give thanks to God for his kindness in providing it. A time of famine, when feasts were often not possible, was believed to be a sign of God's unhappiness with the people.

Grand feasts and banquets did not happen often as they were expensive and involved a lot of preparation. Preparations for the wedding banquet of King Henry III's daughter, Margaret, to the Scottish King Alexander III in December 1251 took five months! Medieval documents tell us what foods and drinks were ordered for feasts but do not often say who was invited to them. There would have been thousands of guests at royal banquets, with all the important nobles of the land invited. The lord of the manor might invite other nobles, his servants, and the peasants working on his land. At the wedding feast of the Spanish princess Doña Blanca in 1440, Jews and Moors (Muslims) were described as attending the celebrations, showing that it was not just Christians who came to feasts.

Feast preparations were an exciting time, although they were also a lot of hard work. The cooks and servants of large noble households knew the rough quantities of food and drink that would be required from their experience of previous feasts. Apart from making sure enough food and drink were ordered and stored, cooks had to have enough wood and charcoal for the cooking fires and ovens.

The banqueting hall had to be cleaned and decorated with colorful drapes and flags. The utensils people would use and all the serving dishes had to be cleaned and polished and the tablecloths washed and ironed. Trenchers had to be prepared, and they were sometimes colored green, pink, and yellow. Servants often rushed around to set up the tables and benches

This banquet scene has been painted within the initial letter beginning this section of this fifteenth-century manuscript.

in time for the big day. The musicians practiced their music and songs, the acrobats tried out their acts, and the players rehearsed their plays. Every detail would need to be perfect so the host and his or her guests would have a memorable time.

Special Food

The best ingredients that people were able to get hold of were used to create a wide variety of fancy dishes, such as veal custard pie, swan stuffed with goose and duck, almond-fish stew, and fried squash flowers. Dishes came in all shapes, sizes, and colors, some hot and some cold. Guests would be impressed if the food was rare or prepared in an interesting way.

Feasts and banquets usually had three courses. Each course could have between five and twelve different dishes. If a feast was held on a fast day, some guests, such as bishops, would have a separate fish menu prepared especially for them. The master cooks would need to know what foods the host and the important guests liked and disliked and what was best for their health. The upper classes of medieval society believed it was important for each course at a feast to be "balanced." It was thought that all foods were "moist" or "dry" and "warm" or "cold." Therefore, it was important to prepare a mixture of moist, dry, cold, and warm dishes for each course. Everything had to be tasted and tested.

The preserved meats and fish provided salty and smoky flavors. Sugar was as expensive as spices, and many dishes made for feasts included sugar as a sign of the host's wealth and generosity. Fruit, flowers, vegetables, and spices could be "candied," or preserved in sugar. "Succade" was fruit preserved

Troubadours playing music at a banquet, from a fourteenth-century German illuminated manuscript. Above, the lord and lady of the house enjoy a game of chess.

in sugar syrup. Many meat and fish dishes contained a lot of different spices like pepper, saffron, cinnamon, and ginger. Some feast dishes were made to be sweet and sour as well as spicy. Sugar and honey were used for sweetness, and vinegar or "verjuice" added a sour flavor. Huge pies were made with crusts decorated and colored like objects of art. Meat and fish were also jellied and served cold. The jelly was made from boiling up the hooves of animals and was then colored. Less spicy dishes were also important to balance the more spicy ones. A famous medieval pottage called frumenty was made with ground grains like barley and almond milk.

The most important dish of the feast was the roast. Often a whole animal such as a pig or lamb was roasted and stuffed with livers, kidneys, bread crumbs, eggs, and spices. Roast meat and fish were made with lots of spices, breadcrumbs, egg yolks, and almonds. Coloring was a very important part of making a special dish. All kinds of substances were used to add color to food, and different parts of the same dish were often colored in white, yellow, red, purple, and green. Rice and almonds were used for white, herbs like parsley for green, sandalwood for pink or red, saffron for yellow, cinnamon for a golden brown color, and other dyes from wood and the roots of plants to give pinks and purples. Real flowers were also used as decorations on dishes. Dishes would have been served with lots of bread and different sauces. Fine wine from Bordeaux in France would have been drunk. After the meal, mulled wine and candied dried fruit were served.

Ceremony and Entertainment

 feast could last a whole day from one morning to the next morning. Large feasts and banquets were like festivals and could take many days. They were usually the high points in medieval people's lives, and they would come wearing their best clothes and shoes.

Feasts and banquets happened at important times of the year, such as the religious festivals of Christmas and Easter, or to celebrate turning points in the farming year such as the harvest or the sheep shearing, when all the wool from sheep was collected to be made into cloth. A city or village celebrated the feast day of its patron saint, usually the saint of the main church in the village or city. Wealthy people held feasts to celebrate a good day's hunting, becoming a knight, or when a new building was finished. Sir Jean Froissart, a French chronicler, wrote in 1385 of the feast that the king of Portugal hosted when he wanted to persuade English nobles to support him in his war against the Spanish rulers.

Weddings and funerals were also important occasions for a feast. The host and guests of a funeral feast were expected to give alms to the poor in memory of the dead

A fourteenth-century Italian painting depicts a royal banquet. The room is filled with servants and musicians, and a religious scene has been placed at the left of the painting.

person. It was normal for a man getting married in an English village to host a feast for his fellow workers. "Bride ale" was brewed for the occasion and had to be paid for by the guests. The bride received the profits from all the ale sold. "Help ale" was brewed to help needy persons by giving them the money from the sale of the ale.

aurum: opera manuum

In an illustration from the *Luttrell Psalter,* pigs are roasted on the spit.

Feasts and banquets were times of great ceremony, especially if an oath was being sworn or a contract signed. The host and the honored guests sat at a "high table" so they could clearly see all the other guests and the entertainment. The host or his guest sometimes sat on a special seat covered with a canopy so everyone knew whose feast it was. Everyone else sat in relation to their social status. Bishops and nobles sat nearer to the host than people of lesser rank, such as merchants, craftsmen, and peasants, who sat at the "low tables," far from the host.

A grand feast or banquet would start after the host and guests said prayers at a chapel or at the table. Servants came round with the ewers or aquamaniles, first to the high table so the host and important guests could wash their hands, and then to the low tables. A large towel was ceremoniously

This manuscript illumination depicts Sir Geoffrey Luttrell and members of his family at a medieval banquet. Two Dominican friars sit at the left. Note the use of plates, knives, and spoons, indicating the family's wealth. Forks were not used at this time.

draped over the tables while the hand-washing was going on. The towel was removed before the arrival of the first course. The start of the eating and drinking was signaled with trumpet fanfares and drumrolls.

At feasts of great aristocrats or royalty, the meals were brought to the table by young noblemen from other households who were learning what it was like to be a great noble. The cupbearer brought the first drink to the host, but it was tasted first to make sure it was not poisoned. The carver had the important and difficult job of carving the roast meat and cutting the pies. There were many rules the carver had to follow. Only the left wing of a roasted bird was given to the host, served with wine and spiced sauce. Hot meat pies were cut from the edge of the crust, while cold pies were cut from the middle. All dishes were tasted by the servant before the host or his guests ate it. The panter guarded the lord's bread, which had to be presented to him on a special cloth. The butler was in charge of the wine and ale. Other servants had special roles, too, and were all dressed in the colors of the noble household.

The giving of gifts was also a great part of the ceremony. There would be time in the celebrations when guests could present gifts. This also gave them a chance to show off by giving unusual and exotic gifts. During a feast in 1326 in honor of the knighthood of an Italian noble's son, he was given two peacocks, two partridges, two pheasants, and two enormous marzipan cakes. The monks who attended this feast were also given gifts of meat, bread, and wine. Giving gifts to people of the church was often expected at banquets.

Feasts frequently ended with cheese and small cakes and sweet or mulled wine or ale. Candied spices were provided as they helped people's digestion.

Entertainment

Grand feasts and banquets were not only opportunities to enjoy good food, but they were also good shows. People came to watch even if they were not invited to eat and drink. Troubadours played flutes, drums, harps, lutes, fiddles, bagpipes, and medieval instruments called hurdy-gurdies. Minstrels sang songs to entertain the guests. The songs told

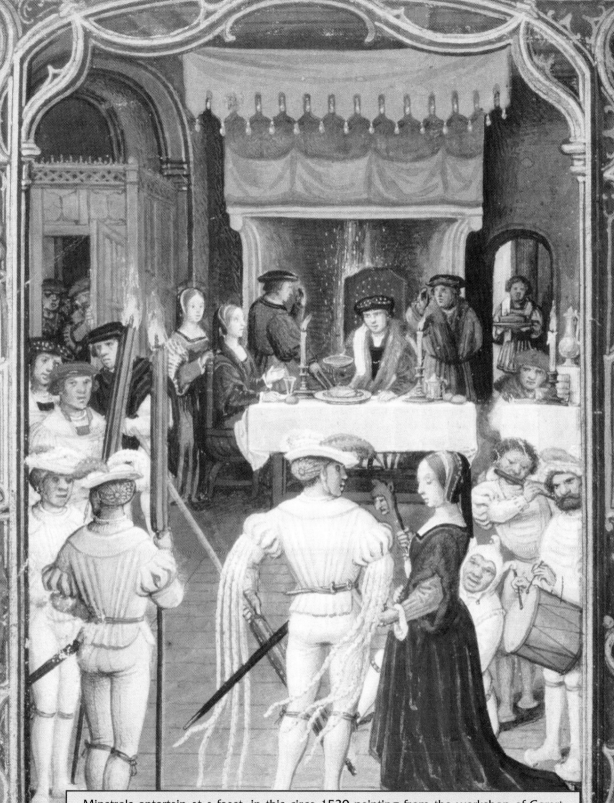

Minstrels entertain at a feast, in this circa 1520 painting from the workshop of Gerart Horenbout and Simon Bening.

stories about eating and drinking or romance. Music was also used to herald the end of one course and the beginning of another.

Between each course there would be a time when people could really enjoy the entertainment. There were plays, masquerades, and make-believe combats like jousts, and people read poetry and stories. Jugglers and acrobats astonished the guests with their tricks and stunts. The guests themselves might be invited to play an instrument or to sing and dance around the tables. These intermissions were called entremets, and small snacks were served during the entertainments. These snacks could be sweet and salted nuts, or "trick food" like fish eggs colored green and disguised as peas.

Perhaps the most spectacular part of grand feasts and banquets were the "subtleties." These combined food, art, and drama. The servants would bring in a platter with a roasted peacock that had all its feathers, wings, and legs carefully replaced to look as if it were alive again. Or a cockentrice might be constructed. This was an animal that was half piglet and half capon. It was meant to create the illusion of being a real animal. Another subtlety was a huge pastry and marzipan castle in all colors. When it was presented to the guests a juggler was seen to jump out of it. When a pie was cut open, guests were surprised to see live birds flying out of it.

How Do We Know?

Historians and archaeologists study what people ate and drank during the Middle Ages by looking at medieval documents, digging up artifacts, or studying surviving buildings of

In this fifteenth-century painting by Jean de Batard Wavrin, the dukes of York, Gloucester, and Ireland dine with King Richard II during his coronation.

the time. There are also many medieval objects in museums around the world that give us information about medieval life.

Many documents that survive were written about royalty and the upper classes of society, so there is more information about the food and feasts of wealthy nobles and royalty than about a peasant's diet. Chronicles were mainly stories about great aristocrats and royalty. These histories can give us information about the grand feasts and banquets that were held. Medieval stories, even though they are fiction, can give us many details about what food was eaten and who ate it, as well as descriptions of feasts.

A banquet scene from a fifteenth-century French painting. The costumes of these diners are particularly luxurious and carefully rendered. A scene of knights in combat has been painted into the background.

There are also many surviving examples of medieval manuals that gave advice on various matters. Manuals were written by people who thought that it was important for certain things to be done in a particular way. There were manuals about farming and how to raise livestock, and manuals for merchants on how to choose good-quality food and spices, for example. There were recipe books containing information about the kinds of dishes that were cooked at feasts and what ingredients went inside them.

Legal documents such as grants for establishing markets or regulations about selling food and drink give us information about where people were able to buy food and drink and also about which foods were important to medieval people. Other laws tell us about the taxes and tolls people paid in food and where hunting was allowed. Household accounts give useful information about the types of food and drink people bought and used for everyday food and for special occasions.

There are many medieval pictures in illuminated manuscripts, on wall tapestries and stained-glass windows, and in early woodcuts and engravings showing people farming, slaughtering animals, cooking food, making wine, and having great feasts and banquets. The pictures of feasts show what food was served, what the guests looked like, the kind of entertainment provided, and the decorations.

When digging at a site where medieval people once lived, archaeologists find evidence of food remains such as oyster shells or cereal grains in cooking pots. This tells us what people ate in a particular place. They also find broken bits of pottery and glass that can be put back together to show us the kinds of things people were cooking with and eating from. Some of these remains can tell us about what ordinary people ate and drank.

Some artifacts have survived in the homes of great nobles and have been passed down, especially precious items like the decorated plates and cups used at great banquets. Goblets, spoons, knives, jugs, and other artifacts can now be seen in museums. Medieval buildings that are still standing also give us information about feasts and banquets. We can see where the great banquet halls were and how big they were or what the kitchens of noble households were like. Historians and archaeologists continue to piece together the evidence to help us learn more about medieval eating, drinking, feasts, and banquets.

Glossary

alms Charity given to the poor and needy, usually in the form of staple foods such as bread. Churches, monasteries, and hospitals, as well as wealthy families, gave alms to the poor.

bottlery/buttery Old English word for a large room, usually underground, in a manor, castle, or palace, used to store wine and ale. The word "buttery" comes from "butt," meaning a barrel.

buttermilk The milky liquid that remains when the thick cream from fresh milk is churned into butter. It can be drunk on its own or used in cooking as an ingredient.

capon A young rooster, a male chicken. Capons are often eaten, as they do not produce eggs like female hens.

chronicler Someone who wrote the histories of nations, wars, royalty, or great families. The document written is called a chronicle.

coat of arms The badge a noble family is granted when it is made noble by the king or queen.

cookshop A place where people could buy ready-made foods.

Medieval Feasts and Banquets

earthenware   A type of pottery made from clay.

elite   Those who had the power to rule over a region, town, or city. Usually made up of nobles, rich merchants, bishops, and their families.

entremets   The intermission between courses at a feast. The light snacks that were served during the intermission were also called entremets.

ewer   A jug for water used at feasts and banquets to wash hands.

fast days   Days when meat or dairy products, such as eggs and cheese, could not be eaten by Christians.

fodder   Food used to feed livestock animals, such as horses, cows, sheep, and goats. Fodder usually was a type of grain or bean that people did not eat except in times of famine.

household accounts   Records kept of what large noble or merchant households bought and used for the running of the household. These accounts included how much the servants cost and the price of buying food and drink.

hurdy-gurdy   A medieval stringed instrument shaped like a lute or guitar. The strings were played by turning a wheel at the side of the instrument.

lard   The fat from pigs, used for frying.

laypeople   People who were not priests, monks, or nuns.

livestock   Farm animals such as cows, sheep, pigs, and goats.

lute   A small stringed instrument that was plucked like a guitar.

mazer   A small, shallow bowl used for drinking wine and ale at feasts and banquets.

minstrel   A singer or musician who entertained the guests at feasts and banquets.

mulling   Adding spices, herbs, or fruit such as apples to wine or ale.

peasants   Medieval people who worked on the land as farmers.

poaching   Hunting that is illegal.

pottage   A thick soup or stew usually made with vegetables, beans, grain, and sometimes pieces of meat or fish. It was the staple food for most people in the Middle Ages.

saltcellar   A container of salt used at the table.

saucer   A small dish containing the sauces that were served with the meat and fish.

subtlety   The food that was created not only to eat but to entertain; for example, roasted birds that were refeathered to look alive again.

tithe   The tax everyone paid to the church. It was usually a set proportion of what people produced from the land.

toll   A tax that was collected at the gates of a town or city from people who came to trade in the market or at a fair.

trencher   A large slice of bread that was used as a plate at feasts.

troubadour   A traveling musician who played at feasts and banquets.

venison   The meat from a deer.

verjuice   A type of vinegar made from sour grapes.

weir   A barrier like a net or fence placed underwater across a river. Used in the Middle Ages to trap fish.

For More Information

The Columbia University Medieval Guild
602 Philosophy Hall
Columbia University
New York, NY 10027
e-mail: cal36@columbia.edu
Web site: http://www.cc.columbia.edu/cu/medieval

The Dante Society of America
Brandeis University
MS 024
P. O. Box 549110
Waltham, MA 02454-9110
e-mail: dsa@dantesociety.org
Web site: http://www.dantesociety.org/index.htm

International Courtly Literature Society
North American Branch
c/o Ms. Sara Sturm-Maddox
Department of French and Italian
University of Massachusetts at Amherst
Amherst, MA 01003
e-mail: ssmaddox@frital.umass.edu
Web site: http://www-dept.usm.edu/~engdept/icls/
    iclsnab.htm

Medieval Academy of America
1430 Massachusetts Avenue
Cambridge, MA 02138
(617) 491-1622
e-mail: speculum@medievalacademy.org
Web site: http://www.medievalacademy.org/t_bar_2.htm

Rocky Mountain Medieval and Renaissance Association
Department of English Language and Literature
University of Northern Iowa
Cedar Falls, IA 50614-0502
(319) 273-2089
e-mail: jesse.swan@uni.edu
Web site: http://www.uni.edu/~swan/rmmra/rocky.htm

Web Sites

Due to the changing nature of Internet links, the Rosen Publishing Group, Inc., has developed an online list of Web sites related to the subject of this book. This site is updated regularly. Please use this link to access the list:

http://www.rosenlinks.com/lma/feba

For Further Reading

Brandenberg, Aliki. *A Medieval Feast.* New York: Harper and Row, Inc., 1983.

Dawson, Imogen. *Food and Feasts in the Middle Ages.* Hove, England: Wayland, 1994.

Deary, Terry and Martin C. Brown. *The Measly Middle Ages.* New York: Scholastic Paperbacks, 1998.

Hanawalt, Barbara A. *The Middle Ages. An Illustrated History.* Oxford: Oxford University Press Children's Books, 1999.

Kelly, Nigel, Rosemary Rees, and Jane Shutter. *Medieval Realms.* Oxford: Heinemann, 1997.

Langley, Andrew. *Eyewitness Medieval Life.* London: Dorling Kindersley, 2002.

Macdonald, Fiona. *Women in Medieval Times.* London: Belitha Press, 2000.

Macdonald, Fiona. *How Would You Survive in the Middle Ages?* New York: Orchard Books, 1997.

McNeill, Sarah. *The Middle Ages.* Hove, England: Macdonald Young Books, 1998.

Bibliography

Amt, Emilie, ed. *Women's Lives in Medieval Europe: A Sourcebook.* London: Routledge, 1993.

Biebel, Elizabeth M. "Pilgrims to Table: Food Consumption in Chaucer's Canterbury Tales." Martha Carlin and Joel T. Rosenthal, eds. *Food and Eating in Medieval Europe.* London: Hambledon Press, 1998, pp. 15–26.

Black, Maggie. *The Medieval Cookbook.* Paperback edition. London: The British Museum Press, 1996.

Cootes, R. J. *The Middle Ages.* London: Longman, 1972.

Cosman, Madeleine Pelner. *Fabulous Feasts: Medieval Cookery and Ceremony.* New York: George Braziller, 1976.

Dean, Trevor. *The Towns of Italy in the Later Middle Ages.* Manchester, England: Manchester University Press, 2000.

Hammond, P. W. *Food and Feast in Medieval England.* Stroud, England: Alan Sutton, 1993.

Herrin, Judith. *A Medieval Miscellany.* London: Weidenfield & Nicholson, 1999.

Hieatt, Constance B. "Making Sense of Medieval Culinary Records: Much Done, But Much More to Do." Martha Carlin and Joel T. Rosenthal, eds. *Food and Eating in Medieval Europe*. London: Hambledon Press, 1998, pp. 101–116.

Hieatt, Constance B. and Sharon Butler. *Pleyn Delit: Medieval Cookery for Modern Cooks*. Toronto: University of Toronto Press, 1979.

Jolliffe, John, ed. *Froissart's Chronicles*. London: Penguin, 2001.

Lopez, Robert S. and Irving W. Raymond. *Medieval Trade in the Mediterranean World*. New York: Columbia University Press, 1990.

Mead, William Edward. *The English Medieval Feast*. London: George Allen & Unwin, 1967.

Mennell, Stephen. *All Manners of Food: Eating and Taste in England and France from the Middle Ages to the Present*. Oxford: Blackwell, 1985.

Mundy, John H. *Europe in the High Middle Ages 1150–1300*. Third edition. Harlow, England: Pearson Education, 2000.

Origo, Iris. *The Merchant of Prato: Daily Life in a Medieval Italian City*. London: Penguin, 1992.

Platt, Colin. *Medieval Southampton: The Port and Trading Community, A.D. 1000–1600*. London: Routledge & Kegan Paul, 1973.

Redon, Odile, Françoise Sabban and Silvano Serventi. *The Medieval Kitchen: Recipes from France and Italy*. Trans. Edward Schneider. Chicago: University of Chicago Press, 1998.

Scully, Terence. *The Art of Cookery in the Middle Ages.* Woodbridge, England: The Boydell Press, 1997.

Tannahill, Reay. *Food in History.* Revised edition. London: Review, Headline Book Publishing, 2002.

Weiss, Susan F. "Medieval and Renaissance Wedding Banquets and Other Feasts." Martha Carlin and Joel T. Rosenthal, eds. *Food and Eating in Medieval Europe.* London: Hambledon Press, 1998, pp. 159–174.

Index

About the Author

Tehmina Bhote was born in 1978 and brought up in London, England. She now lives in Southampton on the southern coast of England. She studied medieval history and now works to research and widen access to historic collections. Her interests include cookery, gardening, and yoga.

Photo Credits

Designer: Geri Fletcher; **Editor:** Jake Goldberg;
Photo Researcher: Elizabeth Loving